Sermon Digest
Volume 2

Copyright © December 2010
by Troy Lee Shaw, Ph.D.
First Edition

Patmos Isle Publishing
www.troyshaw.com

Sermon Digest: Volume 2

Sermon Digest: Volume 2

TITLE: HOW TO MAKE LOVE LAST (1)

Text: 1 John 2:15-19 Love not the world, neither the things that are in the world. If any man love the world, the love of the Father is not in him. 16 For all that is in the world, the lust of the flesh, and the lust of the eyes, and the pride of life, is not of the Father, but is of the world. 17 And the world passeth away, and the lust thereof: but he that doeth the will of God abideth for ever. 18 Little children, it is the last time: and as ye have heard that antichrist shall come, even now are there many antichrists; whereby we know that it is the last time. 19 They went out from us, but they were not of us; for if they had been of us, they would no doubt have continued with us: but they went out, that they might be made manifest that they were not all of us.

Sermon Outline *(1 John 2:15-19)*
1. Don't mistake the scientific for the spiritual v15
2. Don't think love is physical v15
3. Know you've got too choose v15
4. Beware of the deadly trinity v16
    a. Lust of the flesh (satanic sensuality)
    b. Lust of the eye (seeing what you want)
    c. Pride of life (prestige)
5. Choose forever over the fading v17
6. Act as though this is the last time v 18
7. Have the unction for love v19

We must not embrace the idea that we can make love last forever, we can only create temporary superficial pseudo-love; however if we want eternal love, we must look to our eternal God for everlasting love.

TITLE: HOW TO MAKE LOVE LAST (2)

Text: *1 John 3:13-24 Marvel not, my brethren, if the world hate you. 14 We know that we have passed from death unto life, because we love the brethren. He that loveth not his brother abideth in death. 15 Whosoever hateth his brother is a murderer: and ye know that no murderer hath eternal life abiding in him. 16 Hereby perceive we the love of God, because he laid down his life for us: and we ought to lay down our lives for the brethren. 17 But whoso hath this world's good, and seeth his brother have need, and shutteth up his bowels of compassion from him, how dwelleth the love of God in him? 18 My little children, let us not love in word, neither in tongue; but in deed and in truth. 19 And hereby we know that we are of the truth, and shall assure our hearts before him. 20 For if our heart condemn us, God is greater than our heart, and knoweth all things. 21 Beloved,* *if our heart condemn us not, then have we confidence toward God.   22 And whatsoever we ask, we receive of him, because we keep his commandments, and do those things that are pleasing in his sight.   23 And this is his commandment, That we should believe on the name of his Son Jesus Christ, and love one another, as he gave us commandment.   24 And he that keepeth his commandments dwelleth in him, and he in him. And hereby we know that he abideth in us, by the Spirit which he hath given us.*

Sermon Outline *(I John 3:13-24)*
1. Don't be surprised by others v13
2. Know the difference between life and death v14
3. Embrace eternal life v15
4. Pay it forward v16
5. Be about more than lip service v18
6. Keep the commandments v23-24

A Mighty Fortress Is Our God

A mighty fortress is our God, a trusty shield and weapon; He helps us free from every need that hath us now overtaken. The old evil foe now means deadly woe; deep guile and great might Are his dread arms in fight; on Earth is not his equal.

With might of ours can naught be done, soon were our loss effected; But for us fights the Valiant One, whom God Himself elected. Ask ye, who is this? Jesus Christ it is. Of Sabbath Lord, and there's none other God; He holds the field forever.

Though devils all the world should fill, all eager to devour us. We tremble not, we fear no ill, they shall not overpower us. This world's prince may still scowl fierce as he will, He can harm us none, he's judged; the deed is done; One little word can fell him.

The Word they still shall let remain nor any thanks have for it; He's by our side upon the plain with His good gifts and Spirit. And take they our life, goods, fame, child and wife, Let these all be gone, they yet have nothing won; The Kingdom ours remaineth.

— Martin Luther

TITLE: HOW TO MAKE LOVE LAST (3)

Text: I John 4:7-21 Beloved, let us love one another: for love is of God; and every one that loveth is born of God, and knoweth God. 8 He that loveth not knoweth not God; for God is love. 9 In this was manifested the love of God toward us, because that God sent his only begotten Son into the world, that we might live through him. 10 Herein is love, not that we loved God, but that he loved us, and sent his Son to be the propitiation for our sins. 11 Beloved, if God so loved us, we ought also to love one another. 12 No man hath seen God at any time. If we love one another, God dwelleth in us, and his love is perfected in us. 13 Hereby know we that we dwell in him, and he in us, because he hath given us of his Spirit. 14 And we have seen and do testify that the Father sent the Son to be the Saviour of the world. 15 Whosoever shall confess that Jesus is the Son of God, God dwelleth in him, and he in God. 16 And we have known and believed the love that God hath to us. God is love; and he that dwelleth in love dwelleth in God, and God in him. 17 Herein is our love made perfect, that we may have boldness in the day of judgment: because as he is, so are we in this world. 18 There is no fear in love; but perfect love casteth out fear: because fear hath torment. He that feareth is not made perfect in love. 19 We love him, because he first loved us. 20 If a man say, I love God, and hateth his brother, he is a liar: for he that loveth not his brother whom he hath seen, how can he love God whom he hath not seen? 21 And this commandment have we from him, That he who loveth God love his brother also.

Sermon Outline *(I John 4:7-21)*
1. Know where love comes from v7
2. Know who you know v8
3. Love is manifested through action v9
4. Love will die for you vI I
5. Know when God is present vI2-I3
6. Know where you stand vI6
7. Know the judgment day is coming vI7
8. Know the ingredients vI8
9. Don't be a liar v20
10. Follow the great commandments v2I

Words are great; however love must be more than good diction. We should use God's example to lead us toward active love – as we've been given life through our creator, deliverer, and redeemer.

TITLE: HOW TO MAKE LOVE LAST (4)

Text: Matthew 15:32-37 Then Jesus called his disciples unto him, and said, I have compassion on the multitude, because they continue with me now three days, and have nothing to eat: and I will not send them away fasting, lest they faint in the way. 33 And his disciples say unto him, Whence should we have so much bread in the wilderness, as to fill so great a multitude? 34 And Jesus saith unto them, How many loaves have ye? And they said, Seven, and a few little fishes. 35 And he commanded the multitude to sit down on the ground. 36 And he took the seven loaves and the fishes, and gave thanks, and brake them, and gave to his disciples, and the disciples to the multitude. 37 And they did all eat, and were filled: and they took up of the broken meat that was left seven baskets full.

Sermon Outline *(Matthew 15:32-37)*
1. Have compassion v32
2. Pay attention to the need v32
3. Look at what you have and don't focus on lack v33-34
4. Be thankful v36
5. Embrace a more than enough love v37

Far too often we overlook the opportunity to love, because we overlook each other.

A Mighty Fortress Is Our God

*A mighty fortress is our God, a bulwark never failing;
Our helper He, amid the flood of mortal ills prevailing:
For still our ancient foe doth seek to work us woe; His
craft and power are great, and, armed with cruel hate,
On earth is not his equal.*

*Did we in our own strength confide, our striving would
be losing; Were not the right Man on our side, the Man
of God's own choosing: Dost ask who that may be?
Christ Jesus, it is He; Lord Sabaoth, His Name, from
age to age the same, And He must win the battle.*

*And though this world, with devils filled, should threaten
to undo us, We will not fear, for God hath willed His
truth to triumph through us: The Prince of Darkness
grim, we tremble not for him; His rage we can endure,
for lo, his doom is sure, One little word shall fell him.*

*That word above all earthly powers, no thanks to them,
abideth; The Spirit and the gifts are ours through Him
Who with us sideth: Let goods and kindred go, this
mortal life also; The body they may kill: God's truth
abideth still, His kingdom is forever. – Martin Luther*

TITLE: HOW TO BE REVIVED

Text: Jeremiah 3:11-25 And the LORD said unto me, The backsliding Israel hath justified herself more than treacherous Judah. 12 Go and proclaim these words toward the north, and say, Return, thou backsliding Israel, saith the LORD; and I will not cause mine anger to fall upon you: for I am merciful, saith the LORD, and I will not keep anger for ever. 13 Only acknowledge thine iniquity, that thou hast transgressed against the LORD thy God, and hast scattered thy ways to the strangers under every green tree, and ye have not obeyed my voice, saith the LORD. 14 Turn, O backsliding children, saith the LORD; for I am married unto you: and I will take you one of a city, and two of a family, and I will bring you to Zion: 15 And I will give you pastors according to mine heart, which shall feed you with knowledge and understanding. 16 And it shall come to pass, when ye be multiplied and increased in the land, in those days, saith the LORD, they shall say no more, The ark of the covenant of the LORD: neither shall it come to mind: neither shall they remember it; neither shall they visit it; neither shall that be done any more. 17 At that time they shall call Jerusalem the throne of the LORD; and all the nations shall be gathered unto it, to the name of the LORD, to Jerusalem: neither shall they walk any more after the imagination of their evil heart. 18 In those days the house of Judah shall walk with the house of Israel, and they shall come together out of the land of the north to the land that I have given for an inheritance unto your fathers. 19 But I said, How shall I put thee among the children, and give thee a pleasant land, a goodly heritage of the hosts of nations? and I said, Thou shalt call me, My father; and shalt not turn away from me. 20 Surely as a wife treacherously departeth from her husband, so have ye dealt treacherously with me, O house of Israel, saith the LORD. 21 A voice was heard upon the high places, weeping and supplications of the children of Israel: for they have perverted their way, and they have forgotten the LORD their God. 22 Return, ye backsliding children, and I will heal your backslidings. Behold, we come unto thee; for thou art the LORD our God. 23 Truly in vain is salvation hoped for from the hills, and from the multitude of mountains: truly in the LORD our God is the salvation of Israel. 24 For shame hath devoured the labour of our fathers from our youth; their flocks and their herds, their sons and their daughters. 25 We lie down in our shame, and our confusion covereth us: for we have sinned against the LORD our God, we and our fathers, from our youth even unto this day, and have not obeyed the voice of the LORD our God.

Sermon Outline *(Jeremiah 3:11-25)*
1. Be careful not to justify backsliding v11
2. Know that the Lord is holding back v12
3. Beware of strangers v13
4. Let the Lord move you v14
5. Get fed v15
6. Don't walk in your imagination v17
7. Don't depart from the Lord v20
8. Perverted ways lead to tears v21
9. Get your healing v22
10. Don't seek in van v23
11. Don't let shame eat you up v24
12. Get up and obey the Lord v25

There are times when each of us must press the reset button, as our faith seems to become stagnant. Let us focus upon God's word, as revival comes through the perfect food of life.

Abide With Me

Abide with me; fast falls the eventide; the darkness deepens; Lord, with me abide. When other helpers fail and comforts flee, Help of the helpless, O abide with me.

Swift to its close ebbs out life's little day; earth's joys grow dim; its glories pass away; change and decay in all around I see; thou who changest not, abide with me.

I need thy presence every passing hour. What but thy grace can foil the tempter's power? Who, like thyself, my guide and stay can be? Through cloud and sunshine, Lord, abide with me.

I fear no foe, with thee at hand to bless; ills have no weight, and tears not bitterness. Where is death's sting? Where, grave, thy victory? I triumph still, if thou abide with me.

Hold thou thy cross before my closing eyes; shine through the gloom and point me to the skies. Heaven's morning breaks, and earth's vain shadows flee; in life, in death, O Lord, abide with me.- Henry Lyte

TITLE: HOW TO RESCUE THE FAMILY

Text: Genesis 14:10-15:1 *And the vale of Siddim was full of slimepits; and the kings of Sodom and Gomorrah fled, and fell there; and they that remained fled to the mountain. 11 And they took all the goods of Sodom and Gomorrah, and all their victuals, and went their way. 12 And they took Lot, Abram's brother's son, who dwelt in Sodom, and his goods, and departed. 13 And there came one that had escaped, and told Abram the Hebrew; for he dwelt in the plain of Mamre the Amorite, brother of Eshcol, and brother of Aner: and these were confederate with Abram. 14 And when Abram heard that his brother was taken captive, he armed his trained servants, born in his own house, three hundred and eighteen, and pursued them unto Dan. 15 And he divided himself against them, he and his servants, by night, and smote them, and pursued* *them unto Hobah, which is on the left hand of Damascus. 16 And he brought back all the goods, and also brought again his brother Lot, and his goods, and the women also, and the people. 17 And the king of Sodom went out to meet him after his return from the slaughter of Chedorlaomer, and of the kings that were with him, at the valley of Shaveh, which is the king's dale. 18 And Melchizedek king of Salem brought forth bread and wine: and he was the priest of the most high God. 19 And he blessed him, and said, Blessed be Abram of the most high God, possessor of heaven and earth: 20 And blessed be the most high God, which hath delivered thine enemies into thy hand. And he gave him tithes of all. 21 And the king of Sodom said unto Abram, Give me the persons, and take the goods to thyself. 22 And Abram said to the king of Sodom, I have lift up mine hand unto the LORD, the most high God, the possessor of heaven and earth, 23 That I will not take from a*

*thread even to a shoelatchet, and that I
will not take any thing that is thine, lest
thou shouldest say, I have made Abram
rich: 24 Save only that which the young
men have eaten, and the portion of the
men which went with me, Aner, Eshcol,
and Mamre; let them take their portion.
15:1 After these things the word of the
LORD came unto Abram in a vision,
saying, Fear not, Abram: I am thy shield,
and thy exceeding great reward.*

Sermon Outline (Genesis 14:10-15:1)
1. Don't think government won't fail v10
2. Don't trust goods and groceries v11
3. Don't depend on who you are v12
4. Have some allies v13
5. Know who to arm v14
6. Get it all back v15-16
7. Come back to a clean perspective
   (plain/shaveh) v17
8. Get fed in communion v18
9. Hang out with those who will bless you v19

10. Acknowledge God and bless his vessel v20
11. Keep your word v22
12. Never let your actions praise man v23
13. Speak for resources, and not others v23-24
14. Get yours from God v15:1

Family is a great gift from God and we should be grateful, unfortunately it seems that we have become extremely isolated and self-centered; neglecting the collective strength of familial ties. Although, Abram's nephew departed from him after some contention – Abram did not hesitate to aid Lot in a time of need. We should never completely sever our family connections, as the Lord leads us toward love, forgiveness, and restoration.

TITLE: HOW TO HAVE AN INSEPARABLE RELATIONSHIP, RESCUING OUR YOUTH (KEY VS. DANIEL 6:27)

Text: Daniel 1:3-21 And the king spake unto Ashpenaz the master of his eunuchs, that he should bring certain of the children of Israel, and of the king's seed, and of the princes; 4 Children in whom was no blemish, but well favoured, and skilful in all wisdom, and cunning in knowledge, and understanding science, and such as had ability in them to stand in the king's palace, and whom they might teach the learning and the tongue of the Chaldeans. 5 And the king appointed them a daily provision of the king's meat, and of the wine which he drank: so nourishing them three years, that at the end thereof they might stand before the king. 6 Now among these were of the children of Judah, Daniel, Hananiah, Mishael, and Azariah: 7 Unto whom the prince of the eunuchs gave names: for he gave unto Daniel the name of Belteshazzar; and to Hananiah, of Shadrach; and to Mishael, of Meshach; and to Azariah, of Abednego. 8 But Daniel purposed in his heart that he would not defile himself with the portion of the king's meat, nor with the wine which he drank: therefore he requested of the prince of the eunuchs that he might not defile himself. 9 Now God had brought Daniel into favour and tender love with the prince of the eunuchs. 10 And the prince of the eunuchs said unto Daniel, I fear my lord the king, who hath appointed your meat and your drink: for why should he see your faces worse liking than the children which are of your sort? then shall ye make me endanger my head to the king. 11 Then said Daniel to Melzar, whom the prince of the eunuchs had set over Daniel, Hananiah, Mishael, and Azariah, 12 Prove thy servants, I beseech thee, ten days; and let them give us pulse to eat, and water to drink. 13 Then let our countenances be looked upon before thee, and the countenance of the children that eat of the portion of the king's meat: and as thou seest, deal with thy servants. 14 So he consented to them in this matter, and proved them ten days. 15 And at the end of ten days their countenances appeared fairer and fatter in flesh than all the children which did eat the portion of the king's meat. 16 Thus Melzar took away the portion of their meat, and the wine that they should drink; and gave them pulse. 17 As for these four children, God gave them knowledge and skill in all learning and wisdom: and Daniel had understanding in all visions and dreams. 18 Now at the end of the days that the king had said he should bring them in, then the prince of the eunuchs brought them in before Nebuchadnezzar. 19 And the king communed with them; and among them all was found none like Daniel, Hananiah, Mishael, and Azariah:

therefore stood they before the king. 20 And in all matters of wisdom and understanding, that the king enquired of them, he found them ten times better than all the magicians and astrologers that were in all his realm. 21 And Daniel continued even unto the first year of king Cyrus.

Sermon Outline *(Daniel 1:3-21)*
1. Be a choice person v3-16
2. Don't let the meat change you (things of the world and culture) v8
3. Know where your favor comes from v9
4. There is a way out v9-15
5. A divine diet, is better than fleshly fat v12-15
6. Set the trend v16
7. Let God give you insight v17
8. Stand out for the better v18-19
9. Have it all v20
10. Be much better than magic v20
11. Keep on to the next season v21

Text: Daniel 6:3-28 *Then this Daniel was preferred above the presidents and princes, because an excellent spirit was in him; and the king thought to set him over the whole realm. 4 Then the presidents and princes sought to find occasion against Daniel concerning the kingdom; but they could find none occasion nor fault; forasmuch as he was faithful, neither was there any error or fault found in him. 5 Then said these men, We shall not find any occasion against this Daniel, except we find it against him concerning the law of his God. 6 Then these presidents and princes assembled together to the king, and said thus unto him, King Darius, live for ever. 7 All the presidents of the kingdom, the governors, and the princes, the counsellors, and the captains, have consulted together to establish a royal statute, and to make a firm decree, that whosoever shall ask a petition of any God or man for thirty days, save of thee, O king, he shall be cast into the den of lions.*

8 Now, O king, establish the decree, and sign the writing, that it be not changed, according to the law of the Medes and Persians, which altereth not. 9 Wherefore king Darius signed the writing and the decree. 10 Now when Daniel knew that the writing was signed, he went into his house; and his windows being open in his chamber toward Jerusalem, he kneeled upon his knees three times a day, and prayed, and gave thanks before his God, as he did aforetime. 11 Then these men assembled, and found Daniel praying and making supplication before his God. 12 Then they came near, and spake before the king concerning the king's decree; Hast thou not signed a decree, that every man that shall ask a petition of any God or man within thirty days, save of thee, O king, shall be cast into the den of lions? The king answered and said, The thing is true, according to the law of the Medes and Persians, which altereth not. 13 Then answered they and said before the king, That Daniel, which is of the children of the captivity of Judah, regardeth not thee, O king, nor the decree that thou hast signed, but maketh his petition three times a day. 14 Then the king, when he heard these words, was sore displeased with himself, and set his heart on Daniel to deliver him: and he laboured till the going down of the sun to deliver him. 15 Then these men assembled unto the king, and said unto the king, Know, O king, that the law of the Medes and Persians is, That no decree nor statute which the king establisheth may be changed. 16 Then the king commanded, and they brought Daniel, and cast him into the den of lions. Now the king spake and said unto Daniel, Thy God whom thou servest continually, he will deliver thee. 17 And a stone was brought, and laid upon the mouth of the den; and the king sealed it with his own signet, and with the signet of his lords; that the purpose might not be changed concerning Daniel. 18 Then the king went to his palace, and passed the night fasting: neither were instruments of musick brought before him: and his sleep went from him. *19* Then the king arose very early in the morning, and went in haste unto the den of lions. *20* And when he came to the den, he cried with a lamentable voice unto Daniel: and the king spake and said to Daniel, O Daniel, servant of the living God, is thy God, whom thou servest continually, able to deliver thee from the lions? *21* Then said Daniel unto the king, O king, live for ever. *22* My God hath sent his angel, and hath shut the lions' mouths, that they have not hurt me: forasmuch as before him innocency was found in me; and also before thee, O king, have I done no hurt. *23* Then was the king exceeding glad for him, and commanded that they should take Daniel up out of the den. So Daniel was taken up out of the den, and no manner of hurt was found upon him, because he believed in his God. *24* And the king commanded, and they brought those men which had accused Daniel, and they cast them into the den of lions, them, their children, and their wives; and the lions had the mastery of them, and brake all their bones in pieces or ever they came at the bottom of the den. 25 Then king Darius wrote unto all people, nations, and languages, that dwell in all the earth; Peace be multiplied unto you. 26 I make a decree, That in every dominion of my kingdom men tremble and fear before the God of Daniel: for he is the living God, and stedfast for ever, and his kingdom that which shall not be destroyed, and his dominion shall be even unto the end. 27 He delivereth and rescueth, and he worketh signs and wonders in heaven and in earth, who hath delivered Daniel from the power of the lions. 28 So this Daniel prospered in the reign of Darius, and in the reign of Cyrus the Persian.

Sermon Outline *(Daniel 6:3-28)*

1. Have an excellent spirit v3
2. Know that others are waiting for you v4
3. Beware: society will try to steal your worship v10
4. Bow to God, not man v10
5. Be found praying v11
6. Be careful not to do what you cannot undo v14-15
7. Don't expect man's actions to line up with his words v16
8. You may not always know who is praying for you v18
9. Acknowledge the Lord and don't be bitter v20-22
10. Know the power of faith v23
11. The wicked will have their day in the den v24
12. Be a witnesses v25-28

Our children need role models to encourage them toward a life of Christian purpose, whereby they may embrace the Christian culture even when they witness others rejecting God.

TITLE: GODLY RENEWAL (1)

> **Text: Isaiah 40:28-31** *Hast thou not known? hast thou not heard, that the everlasting God, the LORD, the Creator of the ends of the earth, fainteth not, neither is weary? there is no searching of his understanding. 29 He giveth power to the faint; and to them that have no might he increaseth strength. 30 Even the youths shall faint and be weary, and the young men shall utterly fall: 31 But they that wait upon the LORD shall renew their strength; they shall mount up with wings as eagles; they shall run, and not be weary; and they shall walk, and not faint.*

Sermon Outline (Isaiah 40:28-31)
1. Don't forget what you know v28
2. Be aware of God's status v28
3. Know there's more v29
4. Don't think we're exempt v30
5. Learn how and who to wait on v31

Have Thine Own Way Lord

Have Thine own way, Lord! Have Thine own way!
Thou art the Potter, I am the clay. Mold me and make
me after Thy will, While I am waiting, yielded and still.

Have Thine own way, Lord! Have Thine own way!
Search me and try me, Master, today! Whiter than
snow, Lord, wash me just now, As in Thy presence
humbly I bow.

Have Thine own way, Lord! Have Thine own way!
Wounded and weary, help me, I pray! Power, all power,
surely is Thine! Touch me and heal me, Savior divine.

Have Thine own way, Lord! Have Thine own way!
Hold o'er my being absolute sway! Fill with Thy Spirit
'till all shall see Christ only, always, living in me.
— Adelaide Pollard

TITLE: GODLY RENEWAL (2)

Text: Luke 6:6-10 *And it came to pass also on another sabbath, that he entered into the synagogue and taught: and there was a man whose right hand was withered. 7 And the scribes and Pharisees watched him, whether he would heal on the sabbath day; that they might find an accusation against him. 8 But he knew their thoughts, and said to the man which had the withered hand, Rise up, and stand forth in the midst. And he arose and stood forth. 9 Then said Jesus unto them, I will ask you one thing; Is it lawful on the sabbath days to do good, or to do evil? to save life, or to destroy it? 10 And looking round about upon them all, he said unto the man, Stretch forth thy hand. And he did so: and his hand was restored whole as the other.*

Sermon Outline (Luke 6:6-10)
1. Don't let a handicap keep you home v6
2. Don't let attitudes arrest your achievements v7
3. Be willing to let God's work be seen v8
4. Beware of mismanaged time v9
5. Go further than normal v10

We must not let depressive seasons destroy us, although it's easy to become spiritually sedentary – we must continue to overcome obstacle through: prayer, Bible study, worship, and fellowship.

TITLE: HOW TO RESCUE THE CITY (1)

Text: Nehemiah 1:2-11 *That Hanani, one of my brethren, came, he and certain men of Judah; and I asked them concerning the Jews that had escaped, which were left of the captivity, and concerning Jerusalem. 3 And they said unto me, The remnant that are left of the captivity there in the province are in great affliction and reproach: the wall of Jerusalem also is broken down, and the gates thereof are burned with fire. 4 And it came to pass, when I heard these words, that I sat down and wept, and mourned certain days, and fasted, and prayed before the God of heaven, 5 And said, I beseech thee, O LORD God of heaven, the great and terrible God, that keepeth covenant and mercy for them that love him and observe his commandments: 6 Let thine ear now be attentive, and thine* *eyes open, that thou mayest hear the prayer of thy servant, which I pray before thee now, day and night, for the children of Israel thy servants, and confess the sins of the children of Israel, which we have sinned against thee: both I and my father's house have sinned. 7 We have dealt very corruptly against thee, and have not kept the commandments, nor the statutes, nor the judgments, which thou commandedst thy servant Moses. 8 Remember, I beseech thee, the word that thou commandedst thy servant Moses, saying, If ye transgress, I will scatter you abroad among the nations: 9 But if ye turn unto me, and keep my commandments, and do them; though there were of you cast out unto the uttermost part of the heaven, yet will I gather them from thence, and will bring them unto the place that I have chosen to set my name there. 10 Now these are thy servants and thy people, whom thou hast redeemed by thy great power, and by thy strong hand. 11 O*

Lord, I beseech thee, let now thine ear be attentive to the prayer of thy servant, and to the prayer of thy servants, who desire to fear thy name: and prosper, I pray thee, thy servant this day, and grant him mercy in the sight of this man. For I was the king's cupbearer.

Sermon Outline (Nehemiah 1:2-11)
1. Be concerned about the brethren v2
2. Go to God even when you are a mess v4-7
3. Don't forget the promises of God v8-11

Our excuses can keep us from fulfilling the purpose that God has for us. Most of the time our situations are best overcome when we help each other; therefore we should not let our self pity provide reasons for our idleness.

TITLE: HOW TO RESCUE THE CITY (2)

Text: Nehemiah 2:1-20 *And it came to pass in the month Nisan, in the twentieth year of Artaxerxes the king, that wine was before him: and I took up the wine, and gave it unto the king. Now I had not been beforetime sad in his presence. 2 Wherefore the king said unto me, Why is thy countenance sad, seeing thou art not sick? this is nothing else but sorrow of heart. Then I was very sore afraid, 3 And said unto the king, Let the king live for ever: why should not my countenance be sad, when the city, the place of my fathers' sepulchres, lieth waste, and the gates thereof are consumed with fire? 4 Then the king said unto me, For what dost thou make request? So I prayed to the God of heaven. 5 And I said unto the king, If it please the king, and if thy servant have found favour in thy sight, that thou wouldest send me unto Judah, unto the city of my fathers' sepulchres, that I may* build it. 6 And the king said unto me, (the queen also sitting by him,) For how long shall thy journey be? and when wilt thou return? So it pleased the king to send me; and I set him a time. 7 Moreover I said unto the king, If it please the king, let letters be given me to the governors beyond the river, that they may convey me over till I come into Judah; 8 And a letter unto Asaph the keeper of the king's forest, that he may give me timber to make beams for the gates of the palace which appertained to the house, and for the wall of the city, and for the house that I shall enter into. And the king granted me, according to the good hand of my God upon me. 9 Then I came to the governors beyond the river, and gave them the king's letters. Now the king had sent captains of the army and horsemen with me. 10 When Sanballat the Horonite, and Tobiah the servant, the Ammonite, heard of it, it grieved them exceedingly that there was come a man to seek the welfare of the *children of Israel. 11 So I came to Jerusalem, and was there three days. 12 And I arose in the night, I and some few men with me; neither told I any man what my God had put in my heart to do at Jerusalem: neither was there any beast with me, save the beast that I rode upon. 13 And I went out by night by the gate of the valley, even before the dragon well, and to the dung port, and viewed the walls of Jerusalem, which were broken down, and the gates thereof were consumed with fire. 14 Then I went on to the gate of the fountain, and to the king's pool: but there was no place for the beast that was under me to pass. 15 Then went I up in the night by the brook, and viewed the wall, and turned back, and entered by the gate of the valley, and so returned. 16 And the rulers knew not whither I went, or what I did; neither had I as yet told it to the Jews, nor to the priests, nor to the nobles, nor to the rulers, nor to the rest that did the work. 17 Then said I unto* them, Ye see the distress that we are in, how Jerusalem lieth waste, and the gates thereof are burned with fire: come, and let us build up the wall of Jerusalem, that we be no more a reproach. 18 Then I told them of the hand of my God which was good upon me; as also the king's words that he had spoken unto me. And they said, Let us rise up and build. So they strengthened their hands for this good work. 19 But when Sanballat the Horonite, and Tobiah the servant, the Ammonite, and Geshem the Arabian, heard it, they laughed us to scorn, and despised us, and said, What is this thing that ye do? will ye rebel against the king? 20 Then answered I them, and said unto them, The God of heaven, he will prosper us; therefore we his servants will arise and build: but ye have no portion, nor right, nor memorial, in Jerusalem.

Sermon Outline (Nehemiah 2:1-20)
1. Don't be afraid to show your pain to those who can help v1-3
2. Be in a position to ask for favor v5
3. Look ahead v7-8
4. Don't forget man can't bless you, it's God's hand v8
5. Expect help and hindrance v9-10
6. Know the power of 3 days in Jerusalem v11
7. Learn to keep some things to yourself v12 & 16
8. Survey the damage v13-17
9. Know your inner-circle v18
10. Strengthen your hands v18
11. Don't let scorn stop you v19-20

Don't let pride keep you from the promise! Our testimony will often help us and others through the trials of life.

EVANGELISM IN ACTION SERIES

CHURCH EVANGELISM
LUKE 4:33-35

CLEANSING EVANGELISM
LUKE 5:12-16

HOUSE CHURCH EVANGELISM
LUKE 5:16-17-26

HIGHWAY EVANGELISM
LUKE 5:27-32

LIFESTYLE EVANGELISM
MATTHEW 5:13-16

TITLE: CHURCH EVANGELISM: DEALING WITH CHURCHED DEMONS

Text: Luke 4:33-35   And in the synagogue there was a man, which had a spirit of an unclean devil, and cried out with a loud voice, 34 Saying, Let us alone; what have we to do with thee, thou Jesus of Nazareth? art thou come to destroy us? I know thee who thou art; the Holy One of God. 35 And Jesus rebuked him, saying, Hold thy peace, and come out of him. And when the devil had thrown him in the midst, he came out of him, and hurt him not.

Sermon Outline (Luke 4:33-35)
1. Don't get caught up in the voice v33
2. Don't follow the demons instructions v34
3. Don't think demons don't know Christ v34

4. Get them at peace, and get them out v35
5. Don't be surprised at the pitch, hold on to the power v35

Church members must not become so externally focused that we neglect to share the love of Christ internally.

TITLE: CLEANSING EVANGELISM (1)

Text: Luke 5:12-16 *And it came to pass, when he was in a certain city, behold a man full of leprosy: who seeing Jesus fell on his face, and besought him, saying, Lord, if thou wilt, thou canst make me clean. 13 And he put forth his hand, and touched him, saying, I will: be thou clean. And immediately the leprosy departed from him. 14 And he charged him to tell no man: but go, and shew thyself to the priest, and offer for thy cleansing, according as Moses commanded, for a testimony unto them. 15 But so much the more went there a fame abroad of him: and great multitudes came together to hear, and to be healed by him of their infirmities. 16 And he withdrew himself into the wilderness, and prayed.*

Sermon Outline (Luke 5:12)
1. Don't focus on the place (a certain city) v12
2. Don't get caught up in the extent of the pain/problem (full) v12
3. Let Christ be seen v12

Prejudice against people can separate us from the work of evangelism. We must struggle to look beyond a person's situation, in order for us to share the Gospel of Christ.

TITLE: CLEANSING EVANGELISM (2)

Text: Luke 5:13-16 And he put forth his hand, and touched him, saying, I will: be thou clean. And immediately the leprosy departed from him. 14 And he charged him to tell no man: but go, and shew thyself to the priest, and offer for thy cleansing, according as Moses commanded, for a testimony unto them. 15 But so much the more went there a fame abroad of him: and great multitudes came together to hear, and to be healed by him of their infirmities. 16 And he withdrew himself into the wilderness, and prayed.

Sermon Outline (Luke 5:13-16)
1. Don't be afraid to be personal v13
2. Lead others to be a testimony v14
3. Don't get caught up in the fame v15-16

TITLE: HOUSE CHURCH EVANGELISM

Text: Luke 5:16-26 *And he withdrew himself into the wilderness, and prayed. 17 And it came to pass on a certain day, as he was teaching, that there were Pharisees and doctors of the law sitting by, which were come out of every town of Galilee, and Judaea, and Jerusalem: and the power of the Lord was present to heal them. 18 And, behold, men brought in a bed a man which was taken with a palsy: and they sought means to bring him in, and to lay him before him. 19 And when they could not find by what way they might bring him in because of the multitude, they went upon the housetop, and let him down through the tiling with his couch into the midst before Jesus. 20 And when he saw their faith, he said unto him, Man, thy sins are forgiven thee. 21 And the scribes and the Pharisees began to reason, saying, Who is this which* *speaketh blasphemies? Who can forgive sins, but God alone? 22 But when Jesus perceived their thoughts, he answering said unto them, What reason ye in your hearts? 23 Whether is easier, to say, Thy sins be forgiven thee; or to say, Rise up and walk? 24 But that ye may know that the Son of man hath power upon earth to forgive sins, (he said unto the sick of the palsy,) I say unto thee, Arise, and take up thy couch, and go into thine house. 25 And immediately he rose up before them, and took up that whereon he lay, and departed to his own house, glorifying God. 26 And they were all amazed, and they glorified God, and were filled with fear, saying, We have seen strange things to day.*

Sermon Outline (Luke 5:16-26)
1. Must start with prayer v16
2. Don't focus on the day v17
3. Don't be intimidated when the Lord is present v17

4. Find a way in spite of the situation v18
    a. Don't mind their baggage (the bed)
    b. Don't focus on the diagnoses
    c. Don't let even a multitude get in the
       way v19
5. Don't focus on the tilling v19
6. Bring people to Christ as they are v20
7. Be willing to look at the spiritual first v20
8. Know who he is (the sacrificial lamb) v21
9. Choose the hard part v23
10. Let your home bless somebody else's
    home v25
11. Be a witness for the doubtful v26

Christianity isn't just for church; we must be Christians at home also! We should embrace the way of Christ throughout every aspect of life.

TITLE: HIGHWAY EVANGELISM

Text: Luke 5:27-32 And after these things he went forth, and saw a publican, named Levi, sitting at the receipt of custom: and he said unto him, Follow me. 28 And he left all, rose up, and followed him. 29 And Levi made him a great feast in his own house: and there was a great company of publicans and of others that sat down with them. 30 But their scribes and Pharisees murmured against his disciples, saying, Why do ye eat and drink with publicans and sinners? 31 And Jesus answering said unto them, They that are whole need not a physician; but they that are sick. 32 I came not to call the righteous, but sinners to repentance.

Sermon Outline (Luke 5:27-32)
1. See the tax man (undesirables) v27
2. Be a leader v27
3. Be willing to be a guest v29

4. Know the sick, but don't embrace
   sickness v31
5. Know your target v32

Wherever we go, people should see God's love through us. Far too often we're only friendly with the people we know and like. We should strive to display love in our workplace and in the marketplace.

TITLE: LIFESTYLE EVANGELISM

Text: Matthew 5:13-16 *Ye are the salt of the earth: but if the salt have lost his savour, wherewith shall it be salted? it is thenceforth good for nothing, but to be cast out, and to be trodden under foot of men. 14 Ye are the light of the world. A city that is set on an hill cannot be hid. 15 Neither do men light a candle, and put it under a bushel, but on a candlestick; and it giveth light unto all that are in the house. 16 Let your light so shine before men, that they may see your good works, and glorify your Father which is in heaven.*

Sermon Outline (Matthew 5:13-16)
1. Be effective, not just present v13
2. Be un-concealable v14-15
3. Shine for purpose (more than social gospel) v16

Holy, Holy, Holy

Holy, holy, holy! Lord God Almighty!
Early in the morning our song shall rise to Thee;

Holy, holy, holy, merciful and mighty!
God in three Persons, blessèd Trinity!

Holy, holy, holy! All the saints adore Thee,
Casting down their golden crowns around the glassy
sea; Cherubim and seraphim falling down before Thee,
Who was, and is, and evermore shall be.

Holy, holy, holy! though the darkness hide Thee,
Though the eye of sinful man Thy glory may not see;
Only Thou art holy; there is none beside Thee,
Perfect in power, in love, and purity.

Holy, holy, holy! Lord God Almighty!
All Thy works shall praise Thy Name, in earth, and sky,
and sea;

Holy, holy, holy; merciful and mighty!
God in three Persons, blessèd Trinity!
- Reginald Heber

THE KINGDOM SERIES

GO AFTER GOD
MATTHEW 13:44-45

WHEN LITTLE BECOMES MUCH
MATTHEW 13:31-32

BE CAREFUL
MATTHEW 13:24-30, 40, 48

Come, Thou Almighty King

Come, thou almighty King, help us thy name to sing, help us to praise! Father all glorious, o'er all victorious, come and reign over us, Ancient of Days!

Come, thou incarnate Word, gird on thy mighty sword, our prayer attend! Come, and thy people bless, and give thy word success, Spirit of holiness, on us descend!

Come, holy Comforter, thy sacred witness bear in this glad hour. Thou who almighty art, now rule in every heart, and ne'er from us depart, Spirit of power!

To thee, great One in Three, eternal praises be, hence, evermore. Thy sovereign majesty may we in glory see, and to eternity love and adore! – Anonymous

TITLE: GO AFTER GOD

Matthew 13:44-45 Again, the kingdom of heaven is like unto treasure hid in a field; the which when a man hath found, he hideth, and for joy thereof goeth and selleth all that he hath, and buyeth that field. 45 Again, the kingdom of heaven is like unto a merchant man, seeking goodly pearls:

Sermon Outline (Matthew 13:44-45)
1. Get the field, get the treasure v44
2. Rejoice for your find v44
3. Give your all to get it v44
4. Know you're seeking something v45
5. Know the pearl takes time v45
6. Give your all to get it v45

Jesus presents similes within these parables that bring us closer to an understanding of life within God's great kingdom. It seems that these parables suggest that we must give all that we have in order to embrace the kingdom. We must recognize that the kingdom is worth our all, even when we can't see the treasure; but we know the value. There are times when we must buy the field to get to the treasure, although we may feel like we don't need the whole field – we can't acquire the treasure without it. Preceding verses give us a glimpse into the field, as Jesus says that there are good seeds and bad seeds planted in the filed – which gives us the assurance that although life may come with negative and positive experiences; there is an ultimate treasure to be obtained.

The parable of the pearl seems to bring us confirmed hope, as a pearl is created through a process turns something unwanted and irritating into something beautiful. God is so amazing, as we are made beautiful through the sacrificial covering of Christ.

TITLE: WHEN LITTLE BECOMES MUCH

Matthew 13:31-32 Another parable put he forth unto them, saying, The kingdom of heaven is like to a grain of mustard seed, which a man took, and sowed in his field: 32 Which indeed is the least of all seeds: but when it is grown, it is the greatest among herbs, and becometh a tree, so that the birds of the air come and lodge in the branches thereof.

Sermon Outline
1. Be willing to move v31
2. Get planted v31
3. Don't let your position keep you from growing up v31
4. Become attractive v32

TITLE: BE CAREFUL

Matthew 13:24-48 *Another parable put he forth unto them, saying, The kingdom of heaven is likened unto a man which sowed good seed in his field: 25 But while men slept, his enemy came and sowed tares among the wheat, and went his way. 26 But when the blade was sprung up, and brought forth fruit, then appeared the tares also. 27 So the servants of the householder came and said unto him, Sir, didst not thou sow good seed in thy field? from whence then hath it tares? 28 He said unto them, An enemy hath done this. The servants said unto him, Wilt thou then that we go and gather them up? 29 But he said, Nay; lest while ye gather up the tares, ye root up also the wheat with them. 30 Let both grow together until the harvest: and in the time of harvest I will say to the reapers, Gather ye together first the tares, and bind them in bundles to burn them: but gather the wheat into my barn. 31 Another parable put he forth unto them, saying, The kingdom of heaven is like to a grain of mustard seed, which a man took, and sowed in his field: 32 Which indeed is the least of all seeds: but when it is grown, it is the greatest among herbs, and becometh a tree, so that the birds of the air come and lodge in the branches thereof. 33 Another parable spake he unto them; The kingdom of heaven is like unto leaven, which a woman took, and hid in three measures of meal, till the whole was leavened. 34 All these things spake Jesus unto the multitude in parables; and without a parable spake he not unto them: 35 That it might be fulfilled which was spoken by the prophet, saying, I will open my mouth in parables; I will utter things which have been kept secret from the foundation of the world. 36 Then Jesus sent the multitude away, and went into the house: and his disciples came unto him, saying, Declare unto us the parable of the tares of the field. 37 He answered and said unto them, He that soweth the good seed is the Son of man; 38 The field is the world; the good seed are the children of the kingdom; but the tares are the children of the wicked one; 39 The enemy that sowed them is the devil; the harvest is the end of the world; and the reapers are the angels. 40 As therefore the tares are gathered and burned in the fire; so shall it be in the end of this world. 41 The Son of man shall send forth his angels, and they shall gather out of his kingdom all things that offend, and them which do iniquity; 42 And shall cast them into a furnace of fire: there shall be wailing and gnashing of teeth. 43 Then shall the righteous shine forth as the sun in the kingdom of their Father. Who hath ears to hear, let him hear. 44 Again, the kingdom of heaven is like unto treasure hid in a field; the which when a man hath found, he hideth, and for joy thereof goeth and selleth all that he hath, and buyeth that field.   45 Again, the kingdom of heaven is like unto a merchant man, seeking goodly pearls: 46 Who, when he had found one pearl of great price, went and sold all that he had, and bought it. 47 Again, the kingdom of heaven is like unto a net, that was cast into the sea, and gathered of every kind: 48 Which, when it was full, they drew to shore, and sat down, and gathered the good into vessels, but cast the bad away.*

Sermon Outline (Matthew 13:24-48)
1. Don't focus on the bad, and ruin the good v24-30
2. Don't grow up to burn up v40
3. Don't get thrown out the net v48

Be a Christian on purpose, we should not leave the most important part of who we are to chance.

He Leadth Me

He leadeth me, O blessèd thought!
O words with heav'nly comfort fraught!
Whate'er I do, where'er I be
Still 'tis God's hand that leadeth me.

Lord, I would place my hand in Thine,
Nor ever murmur nor repine;
Content, whatever lot I see,
Since 'tis my God that leadeth me.

And when my task on earth is done,
When by Thy grace the vict'ry's won,
E'en death's cold wave I will not flee,
Since God through Jordan leadeth me.

He leadeth me, He leadeth me,
By His own hand He leadeth me;
His faithful follower I would be,
For by His hand He leadeth me.

- Joseph H. Gilmore

RENEWED & REFRESHED SERIES

HOW TO DO THE MATH
PHILIPPIANS 3:4-21

GET OVER IT
PHILIPPIANS 4:5-19

Count Your Blessings

When upon life's billows you are tempest tossed,
When you are discouraged, thinking all is lost,
Count your many blessings, name them one by one,
And it will surprise you what the Lord hath done.

Are you ever burdened with a load of care?
Does the cross seem heavy you are called to bear?
Count your many blessings, every doubt will fly,
And you will keep singing as the days go by.

When you look at others with their lands and gold,
Think that Christ has promised you His wealth untold;
Count your many blessings. Wealth can never buy Your
reward in heaven, nor your home on high.

So, amid the conflict whether great or small,
Do not be disheartened, God is over all;
Help and comfort give you to your journey's end.

Count your blessings, name them one by one,
Count your blessings, see what God hath done!
Count your blessings, name them one by one,
And it will surprise you what the Lord hath done.
- Johnson Oatman, Jr.

TITLE: HOW TO DO THE MATH

Text: **Philippians 3:4-21** *Though I might also have confidence in the flesh. If any other man thinketh that he hath whereof he might trust in the flesh, I more: 5 Circumcised the eighth day, of the stock of Israel, of the tribe of Benjamin, an Hebrew of the Hebrews; as touching the law, a Pharisee; 6 Concerning zeal, persecuting the church; touching the righteousness which is in the law, blameless. 7 But what things were gain to me, those I counted loss for Christ. 8 Yea doubtless, and I count all things but loss for the excellency of the knowledge of Christ Jesus my Lord: for whom I have suffered the loss of all things, and do count them but dung, that I may win Christ, 9 And be found in him, not having mine own righteousness, which is of the law, but that which is through the faith of Christ, the righteousness which is of God by faith: 10 That I may know him, and the power of his resurrection, and the fellowship of his* *sufferings, being made conformable unto his death; 11 If by any means I might attain unto the resurrection of the dead. 12 Not as though I had already attained, either were already perfect: but I follow after, if that I may apprehend that for which also I am apprehended of Christ Jesus. 13 Brethren, I count not myself to have apprehended: but this one thing I do, forgetting those things which are behind, and reaching forth unto those things which are before, 14 I press toward the mark for the prize of the high calling of God in Christ Jesus. 15 Let us therefore, as many as be perfect, be thus minded: and if in any thing ye be otherwise minded, God shall reveal even this unto you. 16 Nevertheless, whereto we have already attained, let us walk by the same rule, let us mind the same thing. 17 Brethren, be followers together of me, and mark them which walk so as ye have us for an ensample. 18 (For many walk, of whom I have told you often, and now tell you even weeping, that they are the enemies of the cross of Christ: 19 Whose end is destruction, whose God is their belly, and whose glory is in their shame, who mind earthly things.) 20 For our conversation is in heaven; from whence also we look for the Saviour, the Lord Jesus Christ: 21 Who shall change our vile body, that it may be fashioned like unto his glorious body, according to the working whereby he is able even to subdue all things unto himself.*

Sermon Outline (Philippians 3:4-21)
1. Don't trust the flesh v4
2. Don't get caught in your history v5
3. Examine your gain v6-7
4. Know what your loss is worth v8
5. Know where to be found v9
6. Except the package deal v10
7. Know you haven't made it yet v13
8. Learn to forget, and reach forward v13
9. Stay focused v14
10. Get the revelation v15

11. We know better, let's stay together v16
12. Focus on the right role models v17
13. Don't seek destruction v18-19
14. Know where your journey leads/ends v20
15. God's fashion is always in season v21

Self-examination must be done in prayer through the movement of the Holy Spirit, as we feed upon the Word of God.

Jesu, Joy of Man's Desire

Jesu, joy of man's desiring,
Holy wisdom, love most bright;
Drawn by Thee, our souls aspiring
Soar to uncreated light.
Word of God, our flesh that fashioned,
With the fire of life impassioned,
Striving still to truth unknown,
Soaring, dying round Thy throne.

Through the way where hope is guiding,
Hark, what peaceful music rings;
Where the flock, in Thee confiding,
Drink of joy from deathless springs.
Theirs is beauty's fairest pleasure;
Theirs is wisdom's holiest treasure.
Thou dost ever lead Thine own
In the love of joys unknown. - Martin Janus

TITLE: GET OVER IT

Philippians 4:5-19 *Let your moderation be known unto all men. The Lord is at hand. 6 Be careful for nothing; but in every thing by prayer and supplication with thanksgiving let your requests be made known unto God. 7 And the peace of God, which passeth all understanding, shall keep your hearts and minds through Christ Jesus. 8 Finally, brethren, whatsoever things are true, whatsoever things are honest, whatsoever things are just, whatsoever things are pure, whatsoever things are lovely, whatsoever things are of good report; if there be any virtue, and if there be any praise, think on these things. 9 Those things, which ye have both learned, and received, and heard, and seen in me, do: and the God of peace shall be with you. 10 But I rejoiced in the Lord greatly, that now at the last your care of* me hath flourished again; wherein ye were also careful, but ye lacked opportunity. *11 Not that I speak in respect of want: for I have learned, in whatsoever state I am, therewith to be content. 12 I know both how to be abased, and I know how to abound: every where and in all things I am instructed both to be full and to be hungry, both to abound and to suffer need. 13 I can do all things through Christ which strengtheneth me. 14 Notwithstanding ye have well done, that ye did communicate with my affliction. 15 Now ye Philippians know also, that in the beginning of the gospel, when I departed from Macedonia, no church communicated with me as concerning giving and receiving, but ye only. 16 For even in Thessalonica ye sent once and again unto my necessity. 17 Not because I desire a gift: but I desire fruit that may abound to your account. 18 But I have all, and abound: I am full, having received of Epaphroditus the things which were sent from you, an odour of a sweet smell, a sacrifice acceptable, wellpleasing to God. 19 But my God shall supply all your need according to his riches in glory by Christ Jesus.*

Sermon Outline (Philippians 4:5-19)
1. Be moderate v5
2. Be prayerful v6
3. You don't have to understand v7
4. Think on the good stuff v8
5. Watch your pastor v9
6. Don't get all bent out a shape v11
7. Roll with the punches v12
8. Know your strength v13
9. Don't neglect the afflicted v14
10. Don't cut off communication v15
11. Don't stop because they won't v16
12. Let your account be fruitful v17
13. Keep your mind on God v18
14. The supply is never ending v19

TITLE: HOW TO OPEN THE DOORS OF THE CHURCH

Hebrews 13:9-16 *Be not carried about with divers and strange doctrines. For it is a good thing that the heart be established with grace; not with meats, which have not profited them that have been occupied therein. 10 We have an altar, whereof they have no right to eat which serve the tabernacle. 11 For the bodies of those beasts, whose blood is brought into the sanctuary by the high priest for sin, are burned without the camp. 12 Wherefore Jesus also, that he might sanctify the people with his own blood, suffered without the gate. 13 Let us go forth therefore unto him without the camp, bearing his reproach. 14 For here have we no continuing city, but we seek one to come. 15 By him therefore let us offer the sacrifice of praise to God continually, that is, the fruit of our lips giving thanks to his name. 16 But to do good and to communicate forget not: for with such sacrifices God is well pleased.*

Sermon Outline (Hebrews 13:9-16)
1. Don't be moved by everything v9
2. Be more than a self-serving organization v10
3. Know that an open door works two ways v11-13
4. Work prophetically v14
5. Be thankful v15
6. Be productive v15
7. Be good and please God v16

The church should not have a cover charge – the doors should be open!

God Be With You Till We Meet Again

God be with you till we meet again;
By His counsels guide, uphold you,
With His sheep securely fold you;
God be with you till we meet again.

Till we meet, till we meet,
Till we meet at Jesus' feet;
Till we meet, till we meet,
God be with you till we meet again.

God be with you till we meet again;
Neath His wings protecting hide you;
Daily manna still provide you;
God be with you till we meet again.

Till we meet, till we meet,
Till we meet at Jesus' feet;
Till we meet, till we meet,
God be with you till we meet again.

God be with you till we meet again;
With the oil of joy anoint you;
Sacred ministries appoint you;
God be with you till we meet again.

Till we meet, till we meet,
Till we meet at Jesus' feet;
Till we meet, till we meet,
God be with you till we meet again.

God be with you till we meet again;
When life's perils thick confound you;
Put His arms unfailing round you;
God be with you till we meet again.

Till we meet, till we meet,
Till we meet at Jesus' feet;
Till we meet, till we meet,
God be with you till we meet again.

God be with you till we meet again;
Of His promises remind you;
For life's upper garner bind you;
God be with you till we meet again.

Till we meet, till we meet,
Till we meet at Jesus' feet;
Till we meet, till we meet,
God be with you till we meet again.

God be with you till we meet again;
Sicknesses and sorrows taking,
Never leaving or forsaking;
God be with you till we meet again.

Till we meet, till we meet,
Till we meet at Jesus' feet;
Till we meet, till we meet,
God be with you till we meet again.

God be with you till we meet again;
Keep love's banner floating o'er you,
Strike death's threatening wave before you;
God be with you till we meet again.

Till we meet, till we meet,
Till we meet at Jesus' feet;
Till we meet, till we meet,
God be with you till we meet again.

God be with you till we meet again;
Ended when for you earth's story,
Israel's chariot sweep to glory;
God be with you till we meet again.

Till we meet, till we meet,
Till we meet at Jesus' feet;
Till we meet, till we meet,
God be with you till we meet again.

- Jeremiah E. Rankin